National Drug Control Budget

FY 2017 Funding Highlights

February 2016

Overview

In FY 2017, a total of $31.1 billion is requested by the President to support *National Drug Control Strategy (Strategy)* efforts to reduce drug use and its consequences in the United States. This represents an increase of more than $500 million (1.7 percent) over the enacted FY 2016 level of $30.6 billion.

The Administration's 21st century approach to drug policy works to reduce illicit drug use and its consequences in the United States. This evidence-based plan, which balances public health and public safety efforts to prevent, treat, and provide recovery from the disease of addiction, seeks to build a healthier, safer, and more prosperous country. The FY 2017 drug control funding request recognizes the significant progress made in addressing challenges along the spectrum of drug policy with the significant drug-related challenges that continue to threaten public health and safety. In FY 2017, for the first time, the Administration proposes more funding for demand reduction efforts than those focused on supply reduction.

The *National Drug Control Budget: FY 2017 Funding Highlights* provides an overview of key funding priorities that support the *Strategy* and an overview of all drug control funding by function.

Highlights of FY 2017 Key Funding Priorities

The non-medical use of opioid medications and heroin use have taken a heartbreaking toll on many Americans and their families, while straining resources of law enforcement and treatment programs. New data from the Centers for Disease Control and Prevention (CDC) show that opioids—a class of drugs that includes many prescription pain medications and heroin—were involved in 28,648 deaths in 2014. In particular, CDC found a continued sharp increase in heroin-involved deaths and an emerging increase in deaths involving synthetic opioids, such as fentanyl.

The President's FY 2017 Budget takes a two-pronged approach to address this epidemic. First, it includes $1 billion in new mandatory funding over two years to expand access to treatment and recovery support services for those suffering from opioid use disorder. This funding will boost efforts to help individuals seek treatment, successfully complete treatment, and sustain recovery. This funding includes:

- $920 million to support cooperative agreements with States to expand access to treatment for opioid use disorders. States will receive funds based on the severity of the epidemic and on the strength of their strategy to respond to it. States can use these funds to expand treatment capacity and make services more affordable.
- $50 million in National Health Service Corps to expand access to substance abuse treatment providers. This funding will help support approximately 700 providers able to

provide substance abuse treatment services in areas across the country most in need of behavioral health providers.

- $30 million to evaluate the effectiveness of treatment programs employing medication-assisted treatment under real-world conditions and help identify opportunities to improve treatment for patients with opioid use disorder.

This investment, combined with other efforts underway to reduce barriers to treatment for substance use disorders, will help ensure that every American who wants treatment can access it and get the help they need.

Second, the President's Budget includes an increase of more than $90 million to continue and expand current efforts across the Departments of Justice (DOJ) and Health and Human Services (HHS), to expand state-level prescription drug overdose prevention strategies, increase the availability of medication-assisted treatment programs, improve access to the overdose-reversal drug naloxone, and support targeted enforcement activities. A portion of this funding is directed specifically to rural areas, where rates of overdose and opioid use are particularly high.

Addressing America's Heroin and Prescription Opioid Overdose Epidemic

Reducing Overdoses

Reducing opioid overdoses, to include identifying those at risk of overdose, the signs of overdose, and expanding the use of naloxone, are key pieces of the Administration's strategy to address the opioid overdose epidemic.

The FY 2017 Budget Request for the Substance Abuse and Mental Health Services Administration (SAMHSA) includes $12.0 million for Grants to Prevent Prescription Drug/Opioid Overdose Related Deaths. This program will provide continuation grants to 10 states to significantly reduce the number of opioid overdose-related deaths by helping states purchase naloxone, equipping first responders in high-risk communities, supporting education on the use of naloxone and other overdose death prevention strategies (including covering expenses incurred from dissemination efforts), and providing the necessary materials to assemble overdose kits.

The FY 2017 Budget Request for CDC includes $80.0 million, $10.0 million above the FY 2016 enacted level, for the Prescription Drug Overdose (PDO) Prevention for States program to cover overdoses from opioids and other drugs. This program, which advances and evaluates comprehensive state-level interventions for preventing prescription drug overuse, misuse, abuse, and overdose, is expanding to all 50 states and the District of Columbia in FY 2016. The additional funding will be used to increase uptake among providers of CDC's opioid prescribing guidelines for chronic pain (slated for release in 2016), as well as implementation of a coordinated care plan that addresses both opioid and heroin overdose prevention by improving care for high-risk opioid patients.

The FY 2017 Budget Request also includes $5.6 million in funding for the CDC to address the rising rate of heroin-related overdose deaths by working to collect near real-time emergency department data and higher quality and timely mortality data by rapidly integrating death certificate and toxicology information. Apart from these programs, the FY 2017 budget request continues to provide funding for expansion of electronic death reporting to provide faster, better quality data on deaths of public health importance, including prescription drug overdose deaths.

Enhancing Prescription Drug Monitoring Programs

Prescription Drug Monitoring Programs (PDMPs) are an important state-based health care tool. PDMPs provide information to health care providers so they can better understand what is being prescribed and intervene before a prescription drug abuse disorder becomes chronic. Currently, Prescription Drug Monitoring Programs exist in 49 states.

The FY 2017 request for the DOJ includes $12.0 million for state grants to enhance the capacity of regulatory and law enforcement agencies to collect and analyze controlled substance prescription data. The objectives of the Hal Rogers Prescription Drug Monitoring Grant Program include building a data collection and analysis system at the state level, enhancing the capacity of existing programs to analyze and use the data collected, facilitating the exchange of collected prescription data among states, and assessing the efficiency and effectiveness of the programs funded under this initiative.

The FY 2017 Budget for SAMHSA includes $119.5 million for the Strategic Prevention Framework. Within this amount, SAMHSA will target $10 million to address prescription drug (including opioids) abuse and misuse; use PDMP data for prevention planning; and implement evidence-based practices and/or environmental strategies aimed at reducing prescription drug abuse and misuse.

The FY 2017 President's Budget also requests $5.0 million in new funding for the Office of the National Coordinator for Health Information Technology to enhance prescription drug monitoring.

Expanding Medication-Assisted Treatment

Medication-Assisted Treatment (MAT) is an evidence-based treatment for individuals with opioid use disorders. However, it is underutilized and often not available to those who could benefit from its administration. Expanding access to MAT, in combination with other behavioral health care, will help address this issue and help more individuals sustain their recovery from opioid use disorders.

Medication-Assisted Treatment Programs

The FY 2017 Budget includes $50.1 million for SAMHSA, an increase of $25.1 million, to support the MAT for Prescription Drug and Opioid Addiction program for states. In FY 2017, SAMHSA plans to expand and enhance its program to improve access to MAT services for treating opioid use disorders. SAMHSA anticipates 23 new states that have demonstrated a dramatic increase in treatment admissions for opioid use disorders will be funded under the FY 2017 request.

SAMHSA is also requesting $10.0 million for a buprenorphine prescribing authority demonstration project that will test the safety and effectiveness of expanding eligible prescribers of the medication to include non-physicians where permissible under state law. For people with opioid use disorders, access to providers of DATA-waived physicians is a significant barrier to buprenorphine maintenance therapy.

The Agency for Healthcare Research and Quality budget includes $3.3 million in FY 2017 to provide a more robust review of evidence and evaluation regarding MAT in primary care settings and to develop and test new methods, processes, and tools for better implementing these treatment strategies.

Medication Assisted Treatment for individuals in the Criminal Justice System

The Bureau of Prisons' (BOP) budget contains $118.1 million, $1.5 million over the FY 2016 enacted level, to support substance use disorder treatment and education. These funds will be used for the Residential Drug Abuse Treatment Program.

The BOP's budget also contains $1.0 million in new resources to expand the MAT Pilot. The pilot will provide an opportunity to evaluate whether MAT should be expanded in the corrections setting.

Second Chance Act Program

DOJ is requesting $50 million in drug-related funding for the Second Chance Act (SCA) Program for FY 2017, $16 million above the FY 2016 drug-related funding level. In an effort to curb recidivism and assist formerly incarcerated individuals returning to communities, the SCA program provides grants to develop and expand offender reentry programs. SCA supports state, local, and tribal governments' and nonprofit organizations' efforts to offer substance abuse treatment and various services to help offenders transition from incarceration to reintegration into society safely and successfully.

Residential Substance Abuse Treatment

The Office of Justice Program's budget contains $14.0 million, $2.0 million over the FY 2016 enacted level, to establish and improve residential substance abuse treatment programs in correctional facilities, as well as community-based services for probationers and parolees in an effort to help offenders stay drug-free and develop skills needed to sustain themselves upon reentry into society.

Drug Prevention

Drug Free Communities Program

The Drug Free Communities (DFC) Support Program is built upon the idea that local problems require local solutions. DFC funding provides for the bolstering of community infrastructure to support environmental prevention strategies to be planned, implemented, and evaluated in communities across the United States, Territories and Protectorates. The DFC Program is guided by local communities who identify and develop evidence-based strategies to reduce drug use and its consequences. For FY 2017, $88.5 million will fund approximately 635 DFC grants and continue the DFC National Cross-Site Evaluation.

Addressing Domestic and Transnational Organized Crime

The Obama Administration will also employ tools to disrupt the flow of illicit drugs into our country, and reduce drug trafficking domestically.

High Intensity Drug Trafficking Areas Program

The High Intensity Drug Trafficking Areas (HIDTA) program, created by Congress with the Anti-Drug Abuse Act of 1988, provides assistance to Federal, state, local, and tribal law enforcement agencies operating in areas determined to be critical drug-trafficking regions of the United States. A total of $196.4 million is requested for the HIDTA program in FY 2017.

Department of Justice Heroin Enforcement Groups

The Drug Enforcement Administration (DEA) is in the forefront of combatting the trafficking of illicit substances domestically and abroad. To strengthen these efforts, the FY 2017 request includes $12.5 million to create four new enforcement groups in DEA's domestic field divisions reporting heroin as the highest drug threat. Funding will provide DEA with additional staff to respond to the increasing heroin threat.

FY 2017 Budget by Function and Other Funding Priorities

The consolidated National Drug Control Budget details agency resources by function. Functions categorize the activities of agencies into common drug control areas. Figure 1 details funding by function.

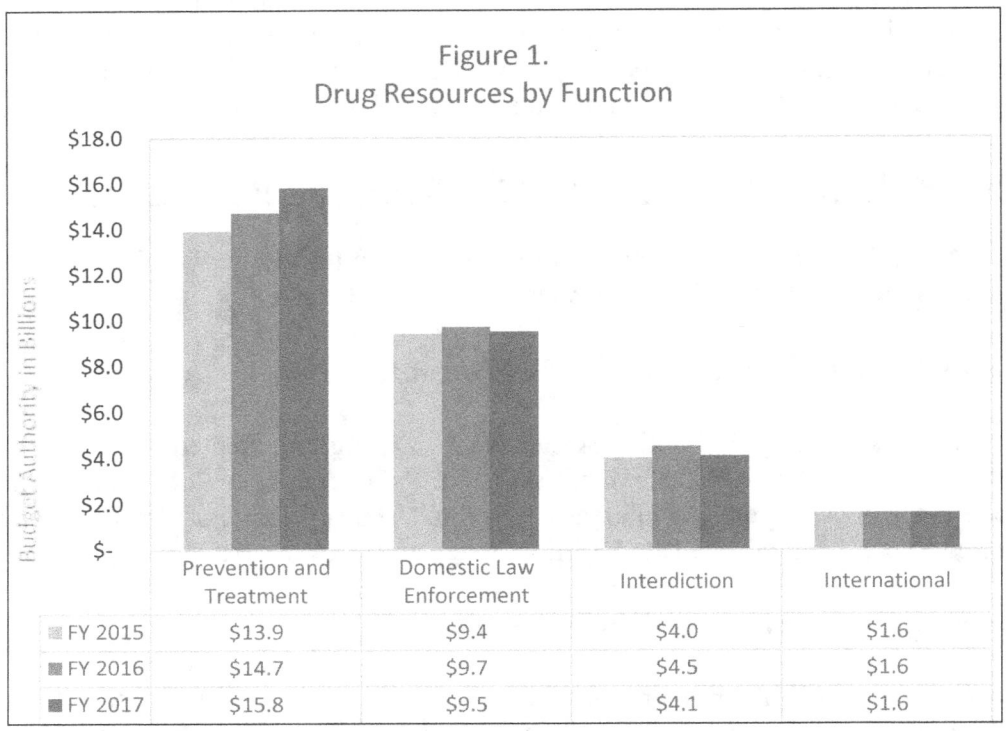

Figure 1.
Drug Resources by Function

	Prevention and Treatment	Domestic Law Enforcement	Interdiction	International
FY 2015	$13.9	$9.4	$4.0	$1.6
FY 2016	$14.7	$9.7	$4.5	$1.6
FY 2017	$15.8	$9.5	$4.1	$1.6

Prevention

Preventing drug use before it starts is a fundamental element of the *Strategy*. Federal resources totaling $1.5 billion in support of education and outreach programs is requested to educate young people about the consequences of drug use and prevent youth initiation. This represents an increase of $48.5 million (3.2 percent) over the FY 2016 level; the major efforts are highlighted below:

> **Substance Abuse Prevention and Treatment Block Grant ($371.6 million)**
> *Department of Health and Human Services – Substance Abuse and Mental Health Services Administration*
> Twenty percent of the $1.9 billion (i.e., $371.6 million) Substance Abuse Prevention and Treatment Block Grant is the minimum set aside to support prevention services. State Substance Abuse Administering Agencies (SSA) use these funds to develop infrastructure and capacity specific to substance use disorder prevention. Some SSAs rely heavily on the 20 percent set-aside to fund prevention, target gaps in prevention services, and enhance existing program efforts.

Education's Prevention Efforts ($50.1 million)
Department of Education
The $50.1 million request includes $46.5 million for School Climate Transformation Grants and related technical assistance. These funds help create positive school climates through multi-tiered decision-making frameworks that guide the selection, integration, and implementation of the best evidence-based behavioral practices. A key aspect of this multi-tiered approach is that it provides differing levels of support and interventions to students based on their needs. In schools where these frameworks are implemented well, there is evidence that youth risk factors are improved; improved risk factors are correlated with reduced drug use, among other improved behaviors.

Prevention Research ($405.9 million)
Department of Health and Human Services – National Institutes of Health
The National Institutes of Health's (NIH's) National Institute on Drug Abuse (NIDA) invests in genetics, neuroscience, pharmacotherapy, and behavioral and health services research, producing innovative strategies for preventing substance use disorders. In addition, NIDA is supporting research to better understand the impact of changes in state policies related to marijuana. Through the National Institute on Alcohol Abuse and Alcoholism (NIAAA), the NIH helps to develop strategies to prevent the short- and long-term consequences of alcohol use among youth.

Drugged Driving ($11.5 million)
Department of Transportation, National Highway Traffic Safety Administration
Department of Transportation, National Highway Traffic Safety Administration's (NHTSA's) FY 2017 request supports the Drug-Impaired Driving Program, which provides public information, outreach efforts, and improved law enforcement training to help reduce drugged driving. Funding will also allow NHTSA to continue to conduct research designed to reduce the incidence of drug-impaired driving.

Anti-Doping Activities/World Anti-Doping Agency Dues ($10.0 million)
Office of National Drug Control Policy
Anti-doping activities focus on efforts to educate athletes on the dangers of drug use, eliminate doping in amateur athletic competitions, and rely on standards established and recognized by the United States Olympic Committee. Funding for both of these efforts promotes an increased awareness in the United States and internationally of the health and ethical dangers of illicit drug use and doping in sport. Funding and participation in the Anti-Doping Activities/World Anti-Doping Agency is necessary to compete in international events. These activities support state-of-the-art research within the scientific and public health communities, while striving to protect athletes' fundamental rights to participate in drug-free sports, and thus promote the health and safety of athletes at all levels.

Treatment

Treatment and recovery support services are essential elements of the *Strategy's* efforts to support long-term recovery among people with substance use disorders. The FY 2017 Budget proposes $14.3 billion, an increase of $1,033.0 million (7.8 percent) over the FY 2016 enacted level in Federal funds for early intervention, treatment, and recovery services. Substance use disorder treatment services need to be integrated better into primary care settings, made more widely accessible, and made eligible for insurance coverage on par with other medical conditions. The Affordable Care Act helped address these issues, but greater attention is needed for the treatment of opioid use disorders in particular. The major efforts in this area include the following:

Medicare- & Medicaid-funded Substance Abuse Treatment Services ($9,140.0 million)
Department of Health and Human Services – Centers for Medicare & Medicaid Services
Substance use disorder treatment is usually financed through a variety of-public and private sources (i.e., private health insurance, Medicaid, Medicare, state and local funds, and other Federal support). The Federal Government makes its largest contribution to the payment for treatment through the Medicaid and Medicare programs. The Medicaid estimate is based on Federal reimbursement to states for substance use disorder treatment services. Medicare supports treatment for substance use disorders in both inpatient and outpatient settings.

Substance Abuse Treatment for Veterans ($707.6 million)
Department of Veterans Affairs – Veterans Health Administration
The Department of Veterans Affairs operates a national network of substance use disorder treatment programs located in the Department's medical centers, residential rehabilitation facilities, and outpatient clinics. It provides effective, safe, efficient, recovery-oriented, and compassionate care for Veterans with substance use disorders and mental illness.

State Cooperative Agreements for Expanding MAT ($460.0 million)
Department of Health and Human Services – Substance Abuse and Mental Health Services Administration
To better address the opioid crisis affecting the Nation, HHS is including a new program to help expand access to treatment for opioid use disorders. The State Targeted Response Cooperative Agreements will be used to assist states in addressing commonly-cited barriers to receiving treatment, such as expanding access, reducing costs, engaging patients, and addressing stigma. It is anticipated that all states will receive some funding to expand treatment for opioid use disorders, but the greater proportion of funding will go to states with the greatest need for additional treatment and the strongest plans for addressing this need.

Cohort Monitoring and Evaluation of MAT Outcomes ($15.0 million)
Department of Health and Human Services – Substance Abuse and Mental Health Services Administration
This new program will evaluate the effectiveness of medication-assisted treatment programs to improve service delivery and decrease the incidence of opioid-related overdose and death.

National Health Service Corps – MAT ($25.0 million)
Department of Health and Human Services – Health Resources and Services Administration
The Health Resources and Services Administration provides medical services to areas of high need, and the National Health Service Corps constitutes a substantial part of this workforce. In order to integrate treatment for substance use disorders into primary care in Corps-served areas, a new request is being made to encourage and incentivize training in the administration of medication-assisted treatment.

Substance Abuse Prevention and Treatment Block Grant ($1,486.5 million)
Department of Health and Human Services – Substance Abuse and Mental Health Services Administration
Up to 80 percent of the $1.9 billion Substance Abuse Prevention and Treatment Block Grant (i.e., $1,486.5 million) is estimated to support treatment services and related activities. This formula-based funding to states supports the provision of substance use disorder treatment services, providing maximum flexibility to states to respond to their local and/or regional emergent issues impacting health, public health, and public safety through a consistent Federal funding stream. The grant allows states to provide a range of clinical and recovery support services to clients during treatment and recovery, and also supports planning, coordination, needs assessment, and quality assurance.

Screening, Brief Intervention, and Referral to Treatment ($30.0 million)
Department of Health and Human Services – Substance Abuse and Mental Health Services Administration
The Screening, Brief Intervention, and Referral to Treatment program, funded via Public Health Service Evaluation funds, provides grants to health care providers to intervene early in the disease process before individuals achieve dependency, and to motivate the clients with substance use disorders to engage in substance use disorder treatment. Grant funds will further integrate Screening, Brief Intervention, and Referral to Treatment within medical treatment settings to provide early identification and intervention to at-risk individuals within the context of their primary care provider.

Treatment Research ($689.9 million)
Department of Health and Human Services – National Institutes of Health
The NIH's NIDA invests in genetics, neuroscience, pharmacotherapy, and behavioral and health services research, producing innovative strategies for treating substance use disorders. For example, NIDA supports a large research network for conducting studies related to treatment of substance use disorders in the criminal justice system, including studies that pertain to the implementation of medication-assisted treatment and seek, test, treat, and retain for individuals with substance use disorders at risk for HIV. Through NIAAA, the NIH helps to develop strategies to treat the short- and long-term consequences of alcohol misuse among youth.

Substance Use Disorders Treatment for Military Service Members/Families ($75.5 million)
Department of Defense – Defense Health Program
The Department of Defense's (DoD) Defense Health Program provides medical and dental services, including treatment for substance use disorders, for all members of the armed forces to include all eligible beneficiaries, including military family members. In addition to treatment services, the Defense Health Program also conducts Alcohol and Substance Use Disorder research.

Homeless Assistance Grants - Continuum of Care ($589.1 million)
Department of Housing and Urban Development
The *Strategy* calls for Federal support for reducing barriers to recovery from substance use disorders, including lack of housing. For persons in recovery, structured and supportive housing promotes healthy recovery outcomes. The Department's Continuum of Care—Homeless Assistance Grants support efforts to eliminate homelessness by financing local solutions to locate, intervene, and house the homeless population. These programs provide housing and supportive services on a long-term basis.

Drug Courts ($92.0 million)
Department of Health and Human Services - Substance Abuse and Mental Health Services Administration
Department of Justice - Office of Justice Programs
Drug courts help reduce recidivism, provide treatment to individuals with substance use disorders, and improve the likelihood of successful rehabilitation through early, continuous, and intense judicially supervised treatment, mandatory periodic drug testing, community supervision, appropriate sanctions, and other rehabilitation services. HHS ($50.0 million) and DOJ ($42.0 million), work together to enhance court services, coordination, and the substance use disorder treatment capacity of juvenile, family and adult drug courts.

Offender Reentry Program/Prisoner Reentry Initiative ($61.9 million)
Department of Health and Human Services - Substance Abuse and Mental Health Services Administration
Department of Justice – Office of Justice Programs
Reentry grants from HHS ($11.9 million) and DOJ ($50.0 million) provide screening, assessment, and comprehensive substance use disorder treatment and recovery support services for people reentering the community after a period of incarceration, as well as people who are currently on or being released from probation or parole. Reentry programs help make communities safer; assist those returning from prison and jail in becoming productive, tax-paying citizens; and save taxpayer dollars by lowering the direct and collateral costs of incarceration.

Bureau of Prisons Drug Treatment Efforts ($118.1 million)
Department of Justice, Bureau of Prisons
BOP continues to develop evidence-based treatment practices to manage and treat incarcerated individuals with substance use disorders. BOP's strategy includes early identification through psychological screening of individuals entering prison. According to the severity of the disease, BOP provides drug education, treatment for those within the

general population, separate intensive residential substance use disorder treatment and community transition treatment. The request includes $1.0 million to expand BOP's medication-assisted treatment field trial program, which provides medication during the last two months of incarceration and for four to six weeks after release in community custody, a residential reentry center, or home confinement.

Judiciary Treatment Efforts ($196.3 million)
Federal Judiciary
The Federal Judiciary provides for court-ordered drug testing, drug treatment, and supervision of Federal defendants, probationers, parolees, and those on supervised release after incarceration. Funding is used by the probation and pretrial services offices for drug testing and treatment of Federal defendants and offenders. Probation and pretrial services officers have primary responsibility for enforcing conditions of release imposed by the courts and for monitoring the behavior of persons placed under their supervision. With Executive Office of the U.S. Attorneys oversight, officers administer a program of drug testing and treatment for persons on pretrial release, probation, supervised release after incarceration, and parole. The goal is to eliminate substance use by persons under supervision and to remove violators from the community before relapse leads to recidivism.

Domestic Law Enforcement
Federal, state, local, and tribal law enforcement agencies play a key role in the Administration's approach to reducing drug use and its consequences. Maximizing Federal support for interagency law enforcement drug task forces is critical to leveraging limited resources. A total of $9.5 billion in Federal resources are requested in FY 2017 to support domestic law enforcement efforts (including state and local assistance, as well as Federal investigation, prosecution, and corrections), a decrease of $173.6 million (1.8 percent) below the FY 2016 enacted level. The major efforts are highlighted below.

Methamphetamine Enforcement and Lab Cleanup Grants ($11.0 million)
Department of Justice
These grants provide assistance to state, local, and tribal law enforcement agencies in support of programs to address methamphetamine production and distribution. Working with the DEA, funding also supports assistance to state and local law enforcement in removing and disposing of hazardous materials generated by clandestine methamphetamine labs, and providing training, technical assistance, and equipment to assist law enforcement agencies in managing hazardous waste.

Federal Law Enforcement Training Center ($43.2 million)
Department of Homeland Security
The Federal Law Enforcement Training Center (FLETC) is a law enforcement training facility that provides training and technical assistance to Federal, state, local, tribal, territorial, and international law enforcement entities. As part of its curriculum, FLETC provides training programs comprised of drug enforcement activities and drug-related investigations to enhance the qualifications of law enforcement personnel.

Federal Drug Investigations ($3,317.0 million)
Multiple agencies
Federal law enforcement personnel—including those from DOJ ($2,520.9 billion), Homeland Security ($543.0 million), Treasury $95.8 million), DoD ($12.4 million), Interior ($14.9 million), and Agriculture ($11.3 million) - prepare drug cases for the arrest and prosecution of leaders and traffickers of illegal drug organizations, seize drugs and assets, and enforce Federal laws and regulations governing the legitimate handling, manufacturing, and distribution of controlled substances.

Federal Prosecution ($873.8 million)
Multiple agencies
A number of agencies—(including DOJ's Organized Crime Drug Enforcement Task Force Program ($161.4 million), U.S. Marshals Service ($144.3 million), Executive Office of the U.S. Attorneys ($75.9 million), and Criminal Division ($39.9 million), and the Federal Judiciary ($447.7 million)—conduct Federal criminal proceedings against drug trafficking and money laundering organizations. The related costs include salaries for attorneys and other court personnel, defender services, judicial and courthouse security, prisoner security, and other administrative costs.

Corrections ($4,476.3 million)
Department of Justice/Federal Judiciary
The Bureau of Prisons ($3,373.7 million), the Federal Judiciary ($597.1 million), and the U.S. Marshals Service ($505.5 million) conduct activities associated with the incarceration and/or monitoring of drug-related offenders. The request includes funding for the costs associated with inmate care, security and facility maintenance, contracted confinement, and general management and administration.

Interdiction

The United States continues to face a serious challenge from the large scale smuggling of drugs from abroad that are distributed to every region of the Nation. In FY 2017, the Administration's request includes $4.1 billion to support the efforts of Federal law enforcement agencies, the military, the intelligence community, and our international allies to support collaboration to interdict or disrupt shipments of illegal drugs, their precursors, and their illicit proceeds. The FY 2017 request represents a decrease of $341.4 million, (7.6 percent) below the FY 2016 enacted level. The major efforts are highlighted below.

Customs and Border Protection ($2,400.4 million)
Department of Homeland Security
Customs and Border Protection implements border enforcement strategies to interdict and disrupt the flow of narcotics and other contraband across our Nation's borders. The comprehensive interdiction strategy includes the border security personnel at and between ports of entry, detection and monitoring provided by aviation assets, and border security infrastructure and technology.

United States Coast Guard ($1,269.0 million)
Department of Homeland Security
One facet of the United States Coast Guard's (USCG's) mission is maritime interdiction. The USCG functions as the maritime counternarcotics presence in the source, transit, and arrival zones. Their maritime interdiction activities disrupt the flow of drugs into the United States.

Federal Aviation Administration Interdiction Support ($12.6 million)
Department of Transportation/Federal Aviation Administration
Air traffic controllers staffing Air Route Traffic Control Centers monitor the Air Defense Identification Zones to detect possible suspicious aircraft movement. When suspicious movement is identified, the Federal Aviation Administration (FAA) notifies the DEA and USCG of such activity. Upon confirmation of suspicious aircraft movement, FAA controllers support interdiction efforts by providing radar vectors to track the time of arrival, traffic advisory information, and last known positions to intercept aircrafts of interest.

Department of Defense Drug Interdiction ($435.5 million)
Department of Defense
DoD's counterdrug programs detect, monitor, and support the disruption of drug trafficking organizations. Additionally, DoD coordinates interagency resources and force requirements of air and surface assets in the Western Hemisphere Transit Zone.

International

Illicit drug production and trafficking generate huge profits and are responsible for the establishment of criminal enterprise networks that are powerful and corrosive forces that destroy the lives of individuals, tear at the social fabric, and weaken the rule of law in affected countries. In FY 2017, $1.6 billion is requested for international drug control efforts, a decrease of $55.9 million (3.4 percent) below the FY 2016 enacted level. These funds are requested to support the efforts of the United States Government and our international partners around the globe to meet the challenges of illicit trafficking of all drugs, including synthetics and precursors, and illicit substance use. The major efforts in this area include the following.

DEA's International Efforts ($467.9 million)
Department of Justice
The focus of DEA's international enforcement program is to disrupt or dismantle the most significant international drug and precursor chemical trafficking organizations around the world. Personnel in DEA's foreign country offices focus their investigative efforts on the most significant international command and control organizations threatening the United States. DEA coordinates all programs involving drug law enforcement in foreign countries, and also provides intelligence to assist the interagency community in determining future trends in drug trafficking and evaluating their long-term impact. DEA works closely with the United Nations, Interpol, and other organizations on matters relating to international drug and chemical control programs.

Bureau of International Narcotics and Law Enforcement Affairs ($382.4 million)
Department of State
In support of the *Strategy*, Bureau of International Narcotics and Law Enforcement Affairs (INL) works closely with partner nations and source countries to disrupt illicit drug production, strengthen criminal justice systems and law enforcement institutions, and combat transnational organized crime. INL is comprehensive in its approach to the counterdrug mission and provides training and technical assistance for prevention and treatment programs.

United States Agency for International Development ($131.9 million)
Department of State
The United States Agency for International Development (USAID) provides foreign assistance funds to develop holistic alternatives to illicit drug production by providing agricultural assistance, improving small scale infrastructure, increasing market accessibility, and incentivizing licit crop production. USAID's alternative development programs foster economic growth, local governance and civil society strengthening, and enhanced security of impacted communities.

DoD International Counternarcotics Efforts ($567.1 million)
Department of Defense
The international support programs of DoD's Combatant Commands detect, interdict, disrupt, or monitor activities related to drug trafficking organizations and transnational criminal organizations. In the Western Hemisphere Transit Zone, DoD functions as the command and control support for counterdrug activities for Federal, state, local and international partners.

The tables below provide further detail on Federal drug control funding by function (Table 1), Federal drug control funding by agency (Table 2), and historical Federal drug control funding (Table 3).

Table 1: Federal Drug Control Spending by Function

FY 2015 - FY 2017

(Budget Authority in Millions)

	FY 2015 Final	FY2016 Enacted	FY 2017 Request	FY16-FY17 Change Dollars	Percent
Function					
Treatment	$12,543.1	$13,248.6	$14,281.6	+$1,033.0	+7.8%
Percent	*43.4%*	*43.4%*	*46.0%*		
Prevention	1,341.5	1,496.2	1,544.7	+48.5	+3.2%
Percent	*4.6%*	*4.9%*	*5.0%*		
Domestic Law Enforcement	9,394.5	9,699.1	9,525.5	-173.6	-1.8%
Percent	*32.5%*	*31.7%*	*30.7%*		
Interdiction	3,960.9	4,479.9	4,138.5	-341.4	-7.6%
Percent	*13.7%*	*14.7%*	*13.3%*		
International	1,643.0	1,637.0	1,581.1	-55.9	-3.4%
Percent	*5.7%*	*5.4%*	*5.1%*		
Total	**$28,882.9**	**$30,560.8**	**$31,071.4**	**+S510.6**	***+1.7%***
Supply/Demand					
Demand Reduction	$13,884.6	$14,744.8	$15,826.3	+$1,081.5	+7.3%
Percent	*48.1%*	*48.2%*	*50.9%*		
Supply Reduction	14,998.3	15,816.1	15,245.1	-571.0	-3.6%
Percent	*51.9%*	*51.8%*	*49.1%*		
Total	**$28,882.9**	**$30,560.8**	**$31,071.4**	**+$510.6**	***+1.7%***

Note: Detail may not add due to rounding.

Table 2: Federal Drug Control Spending by Agency

(Budget Authority in Millions)[1]

	FY2015 Final	FY2016 Enacted	FY2017 Request
Department of Agriculture			
U.S. Forest Service	12.4	12.3	17.9
Court Services and Offender Supervision Agency for the District of Columbia	52.6	58.1	58.7
Department of Defense			
Drug Interdiction and Counterdrug Activities/OPTEMPO	1,409.3	1,343.3	1,222.0
Defense Health Program	<u>73.5</u>	<u>75.5</u>	<u>75.5</u>
Total DoD	**1,482.8**	**1,418.8**	**1,297.5**
Department of Education			
Office of Elementary and Secondary Education	50.2	50.1	50.1
Federal Judiciary	1,158.9	1,210.6	1,246.7
Department of Health and Human Services			
Administration for Children and Families	18.6	18.5	60.0
Centers for Disease Control and Prevention	20.0	75.6	85.6
Centers for Medicare & Medicaid Services[2]	8,230.0	8,760.0	9,140.0
Health Resources and Services Administration	27.8	129.0	164.0
Indian Health Service	111.3	114.7	140.9
National Institute on Alcohol Abuse and Alcoholism	59.5	54.2	54.2
National Institute on Drug Abuse	1,015.7	1,050.6	1,050.6
Substance Abuse and Mental Health Services Administration[3]	<u>2,460.4</u>	<u>2,512.2</u>	<u>2,986.0</u>
Total Health and Human Services	**11,943.3**	**12,714.7**	**13,681.3**
Department of Homeland Security			
Customs and Border Protection	2,423.0	2,664.9	2,655.7
Federal Emergency Management Agency	8.3	8.3	6.2
Federal Law Enforcement Training Center	46.8	44.1	43.6
Immigration and Customs Enforcement	467.9	485.8	527.0
United States Coast Guard	<u>1,265.7</u>	<u>1,616.1</u>	<u>1,269.0</u>
Total Homeland Security	**4,211.5**	**4,819.1**	**4,501.6**
Department of Housing and Urban Development			
Community Planning and Development	463.5	486.9	589.1
Department of the Interior			
Bureau of Indian Affairs	9.7	9.7	9.7
Bureau of Land Management	5.1	5.1	5.1
National Park Service	<u>3.3</u>	<u>3.3</u>	<u>3.3</u>
Total Interior	**18.1**	**18.1**	**18.1**

	FY2015 Final	FY2016 Enacted	FY2017 Request
Department of Justice			
Assets Forfeiture Fund	284.1	238.7	243.1
Bureau of Prisons	3,491.0	3,672.4	3,491.8
Criminal Division	40.0	39.0	39.9
Drug Enforcement Administration	2,373.1	2,426.5	2,485.6
Organized Crime Drug Enforcement Task Force Program	507.2	512.0	522.1
Office of Justice Programs	260.9	280.2	275.6
U.S. Attorneys	76.8	72.6	75.9
U.S. Marshals Service	270.4	278.1	289.9
U.S. Marshals Service - Federal Prisoner Detention	498.0	510.0	505.5
Total Justice	**7,801.7**	**8,029.6**	**7,929.4**
Department of Labor			
Employment and Training Administration	6.0	6.0	6.0
Office of National Drug Control Policy			
High Intensity Drug Trafficking Areas	245.0	250.0	196.4
Other Federal Drug Control Programs	107.2	109.8	98.5
Salaries and Expenses	22.6	20.0	19.3
Total ONDCP	**374.8**	**379.9**	**314.2**
Department of State[4]			
Bureau of International Narcotics and Law Enforcement Affairs	446.1	434.7	382.4
United States Agency for International Development	95.5	136.2	131.9
Total State	**541.6**	**570.8**	**514.3**
Department of Transportation			
Federal Aviation Administration	30.7	31.5	31.6
National Highway Traffic Safety Administration	2.7	11.5	11.5
Total Transportation	**33.4**	**43.0**	**43.1**
Department of the Treasury			
Internal Revenue Service	60.3	60.3	95.8
Department of Veterans Affairs			
Veterans Health Administration[5]	671.8	682.4	707.6
	$28,882.9	**$30,560.8**	**$31,071.4**

[1] Detail may not add due to rounding.
[2] The estimates for the CMS reflect Medicaid and Medicare benefit outlays for substance use disorder treatment; they do not reflect budget authority. The estimates were developed by the CMS Office of the Actuary.
[3] Includes budget authority and funding through evaluation set-aside authorized by Section 241 of the Public Health Service (PHS) Act.
[4] The FY 2016 funding level represents the FY 2016 President's Budget request.
[5] VA Medical Care receives advance appropriations; FY 2016 funding was provided in the Consolidated Appropriations Act, 2014 (Public Law No 113-76).

Table 3: Historical Federal Drug Control Spending

(Budget Authority in Millions)[1]

	FY2008 Final	FY2009 Final	FY2010 Final	FY2011 Final	FY2012 Final	FY2013 Final	FY2014 Final	FY2015 Final	FY2016 Enacted	FY2017 Request
Treatment	6,725.1	7,208.7	7,544.5	7,659.7	7,848.3	7,888.6	9,481.8	12,543.1	13,248.6	14,281.6
Prevention	1,848.1	1,961.0	1,573.4	1,483.9	1,346.2	1,274.9	1,316.9	1,341.5	1,496.2	1,544.7
Total Demand Reduction	**8,573.2** 39.3%	**9,169.7** 36.9%	**9,117.9** 37.0%	**9,143.5** 37.5%	**9,194.4** 37.5%	**9,163.5** 38.5%	**10,798.7** 42.0%	**13,884.6** 48.1%	**14,744.8** 48.2%	**15,826.3** 50.9%
Domestic Law Enforcement	8,293.9	9,463.0	9,245.5	9,217.3	9,439.5	8,857.0	9,348.8	9,394.5	9,699.1	9,525.5
Interdiction	2,968.7	3,699.2	3,662.4	3,977.1	4,036.5	3,940.6	3,948.5	3,960.9	4,479.9	4,138.5
International	1,998.5	2,532.6	2,595.0	2,027.6	1,833.7	1,848.5	1,637.1	1,643.0	1,637.0	1,581.1
Total Supply Reduction	**13,261.1** 60.7%	**15,694.9** 63.1%	**15,502.9** 63.0%	**15,221.9** 62.5%	**15,309.7** 62.5%	**14,646.1** 61.5%	**14,934.4** 58.0%	**14,998.3** 51.9%	**15,816.1** 51.8%	**15,245.1** 49.1%

[1] Detail may not add due to rounding.